best
easy
dayhikes
Southern
Sierra

Ron Adkison

FALCON®

Guilford, Connecticut

An imprint of The Globe Pequot Press

A **FALCON** GUIDE®

Library of Congress Cataloging-in-Publication data is available.

ISBN 1-58592-049-5

Manufactured in the United States of America
First Edition/First Printing

CAUTION
Outdoor recreational activities are by their very nature potentially hazardous. All participants in such activities must assume responsibility for their own actions and safety. The information contained in this guidebook cannot replace sound judgment and good decision-making skills, which help reduce risk exposure, nor does the scope of this book allow for disclosure of all the potential hazards and risks involved in such activities. Learn as much as possible about the outdoor recreational activities in which you participate, prepare for the unexpected, and be cautious. The reward will be a safer and more enjoyable experience.

Contents

Map Legend

Interstate Highway/Freeway	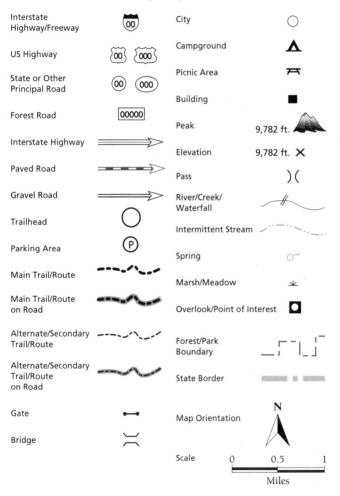	City	○
US Highway		Campground	▲
State or Other Principal Road		Picnic Area	╤
Forest Road		Building	■
Interstate Highway		Peak	9,782 ft.
Paved Road		Elevation	9,782 ft. ✕
Gravel Road		Pass	) (
Trailhead		River/Creek/Waterfall	
Parking Area		Intermittent Stream	
Main Trail/Route		Spring	
Main Trail/Route on Road		Marsh/Meadow	
Alternate/Secondary Trail/Route		Overlook/Point of Interest	
Alternate/Secondary Trail/Route on Road		Forest/Park Boundary	
Gate		State Border	
Bridge		Map Orientation	N
		Scale	0 0.5 1 Miles

Overview Map of the Southern Sierra

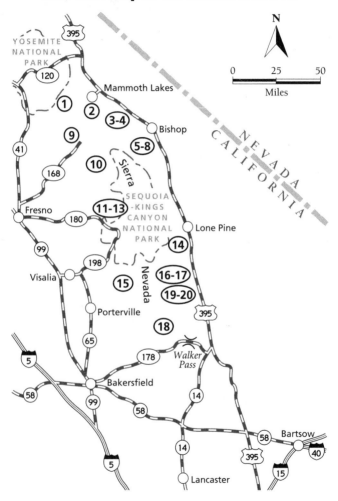

Ranking the Hikes

The following list ranks the hikes in this book from easiest to hardest.

Help Us Keep This Guide Up to Date

Every effort has been made by the authors and editors to make this guide as accurate and useful as possible. However, many things can change after a guide is published—establishments close, phone numbers change, hiking trails are rerouted, facilities come under new management, etc.

We would love to hear from you concerning your experiences with this guide and how you feel it could be improved and kept up to date. While we may not be able to respond to all comments and suggestions, we'll take them to heart and we'll also make certain to share them with the authors. Please send your comments and suggestions to the following address:

The Globe Pequot Press

Reader Response/Editorial Department

P.O. Box 480

Guilford, CT 06437

Or you may e-mail us at:

editorial@globe-pequot.com

Thanks for your input, and happy travels!

Introduction

The Southern Sierra stretches 160 miles, from the southern boundary of Yosemite National Park to Walker Pass east of Bakersfield. Not a single road crosses the range from east to west in the Southern Sierra, in part because of the sheer ruggedness of the region, and also because much of the land here has been designated as wilderness. From the Sequoia National Forest road that links Kennedy Meadows to Kernville on the southern Kern Plateau, a contiguous chain of 8 wilderness areas, encompassing some 2.1 million acres, stretches northward through the heart of the Sierra to Yosemite. Two other wilderness areas, Kaiser and Dinkey Lakes, are separated from the chain of wilderness areas by forest road corridors. Four more wilderness areas, containing another 271,000 acres of roadless lands, are south of the Kennedy Meadows-to-Kernville road and north of Walker Pass.

Not only does the Southern Sierra contain one of the largest blocks of roadless land in the lower 48 states, it also boasts one of the largest contiguous areas above 10,000 feet. In addition, it encompasses Mt. Whitney, at 14,495 feet the highest mountain in the lower 48 states; the giant sequoias, the largest living things on earth; and Kings Canyon, one of the deepest gorges in North America.

The great number of best easy day hikes in the Southern Sierra could fill many volumes of a little book like this. The 20 hikes in this book are purely my biased opinion of the best easy hikes in this region, based on many years of experience and hiking thousands of miles. Not all of the hikes are "easy." The Southern Sierra is a mountainous land, so naturally most hikes are going to go uphill, and hiking here is a little more rigorous than in the gentler Northern Sierra. Many of the hikes are located deep in the mountains, so choosing to take any of them not only offers a memorable hiking trip, but also affords the opportunity for a scenic drive and makes the trips well suited for a weekend outing.

Because most of the short hikes in this book begin at high elevations, the best time to go is in the summer and early autumn. Always be prepared, wear sturdy shoes or boots, carry rain gear, and a good map, and be sure everyone in your group carries one to two quarts of water.

—*Ron Adkison*

Zero Impact

Going into a wild area is like visiting a famous museum. You obviously do not want to leave your mark on an art treasure in the museum. If everybody going through the museum left one little mark, the art would be destroyed quickly—and of what value is a big building full of trashed art? The same goes for pristine wildlands. If we all left just one little mark on the landscape, the backcountry would soon be spoiled.

A wilderness can accommodate human use as long as everybody behaves. However, a few thoughtless or uninformed visitors can ruin it for everybody who follows. All backcountry users have a responsibility to know and follow the rules of zero impact camping.

Three Falcon Zero-Impact Principles
- *Leave with everything you brought.*
- *Leave no sign of your visit.*
- *Leave the landscape as you found it.*

Nowadays most wilderness users want to walk softly, but some are not aware that they have poor manners. Often their actions are dictated by the outdated habits of a generation of campers who cut green boughs for shelters, built campfires with fire rings, and dug trenches around tents. Today, such behavior is absolutely unacceptable. A new code of ethics is growing out of the necessity of coping with the unending waves of people who want a perfect back-country experience. To ensure you leave no sign of your passage, follow these recommendations:

- Be sure you leave nothing along the trail or at your campsite. Pack out everything, including orange peels, flip tops, cigarette butts, and gum wrappers. Also, pick up any trash that others leave behind.
- Follow the main trail. Avoid cutting switchbacks and walking on vegetation beside the trail.
- Do not pick up "souvenirs," such as rocks, antlers, or wildflowers. The next person wants to see them too, and collecting souvenirs may violate regulations.
- Avoid making loud noises on the trail (unless you are in bear country) or in camp.
- Carry a lightweight trowel to bury human waste 6 to 8 inches deep and at least 300 feet from any water source. Pack out used toilet paper.
- Go without a campfire. Carry a stove for cooking and a flashlight, candle lantern, or headlamp for light. For emergencies, learn how to build a no-trace fire.
- Camp in designated sites if they are available. Otherwise, camp and cook on durable surfaces such as bedrock, sand, gravel bars, or bare ground.
- Follow the pack-in/pack-out rule. If you carry something into the backcountry, consume it or carry it out.

Leave no trace—and put your ear to the ground and listen carefully. Thousands of people coming behind you are thanking you for your courtesy and good sense.

Make It a Safe Trip

The Boy Scouts of America have been guided for decades by what is perhaps the single best piece of safety advice— Be Prepared! For starters, this means carrying and knowing how to use survival and first-aid materials, proper clothing, a compass, and a topographic map.

Perhaps the second-best piece of safety advice is to tell somebody where you are going and when you plan to return. File your "flight plan" with a friend or relative before taking off.

Physical conditioning is also important. Being fit not only makes wilderness travel more fun, it makes it safer.

To whet your appetite for more knowledge of wilderness safety and preparedness, here are a few more tips:

- Check the weather forecast. Be careful not to get caught at high elevations by a bad storm or along a stream in a flash flood. To avoid getting stranded on a ridgeline during a lightning storm, watch cloud formations closely. Avoid traveling during prolonged periods of cold weather.
- Avoid traveling alone.
- Keep your party together.
- Study basic survival and first aid before leaving home.
- Do not eat wild plants unless you have positively identified them.
- Before you leave for the trailhead, find out as much as you can about the route, especially the potential hazards.

- Do not exhaust yourself or other members of your party by traveling too far or too fast. Let the slowest person set the pace.
- Do not wait until you are confused to look at your maps. Keep a continual fix on your location by following your map from the moment you start moving up the trail.
- If you get lost, do not panic. Sit down and relax while you check your topographic map and take a compass reading. It is often smart to retrace your steps until you find familiar ground, then plan your next move.
- Stay clear of all wild animals.
- Take a first-aid kit that includes, at a minimum: a sewing needle, a snake-bite kit, aspirin, antibacterial ointment, 2 antiseptic swabs, 2 butterfly bandages, adhesive tape, 4 adhesive strips, 4 gauze pads, 2 triangular bandages, codeine tablets, 2 inflatable splints, moleskin or a similar dressing for blisters, one roll of 3-inch gauze, a CPR shield, rubber gloves, and a first-aid instructional manual.
- Take a survival kit that includes, at a minimum: compass, whistle, matches in a waterproof container, cigarette lighter, candle, signal mirror, flashlight, fire starter, aluminum foil, water purification tablets, space blanket, and flare.
- Last but not least, do not forget that the best defense against unexpected hazards is knowledge. Read up on the latest in wilderness safety information in Falcon Publishing's *Wild Country Companion*.

Maps

Three types of maps are commonly listed in hike descriptions in *Best Easy Day Hikes Southern Sierra:* United States Geological Survey (USGS) topographic quadrangles, national forest maps, and wilderness maps.

The U.S. Forest Service provides maps for each national forest, which are most useful for locating and driving to trailheads. They are available at Forest Service stations.

Most hikers prefer U.S. Geological Survey topographic quadrangles. Topo maps are available at most backpacking and sporting goods stores, and at some national forest and most national park visitor centers, or they can be ordered directly from USGS Information Services, Box 25286, Denver, CO 80225; (888)-ASK-USGS; http://mapping.usgs.gov.

Topographic wilderness maps produced by the Forest Service cover many wilderness areas in the Southern Sierra. These maps are available through the mail by writing the USDA Forest Service, Pacific Southwest Region, Attn: Geometronics, 1323 Club Drive, Vallejo, CA 94592 or in person at appropriate district ranger offices.

You Might Never Know What Hit You

Mountains are prone to sudden thunderstorms. Here are some things to remember if you get caught in a lightning storm:

- Lightning can travel far ahead of the storm, so take cover before the storm hits.
- Be especially careful not to get caught on a mountaintop or exposed ridge; under large, solitary trees; in the

open; or near standing water. Seek shelter in a low-lying area, ideally in a dense stand of small, uniformly sized trees.

- Stay away from anything that might attract lightning, such as metal tent poles, graphite fishing rods, or pack frames.
- Get in a crouched position and place both feet firmly on the ground. If you have a pack (without a metal frame) or a sleeping pad with you, put your feet on the pack or pad for extra insulation against shock.
- Do not walk or huddle together. Stay 50 feet apart, so that if somebody gets hit by lightning, others in the party can give first aid.
- If you are in a tent, stay there. Get in your sleeping bag with your feet on your sleeping pad.

The Silent Killer

Hypothermia—a condition in which the body's internal temperature drops below normal—is caused by exposure to cold and is aggravated by wetness, wind, and exhaustion. If untreated, the condition can lead to mental and physical collapse and death.

If your party is exposed to wind, cold, and wet, think hypothermia. Watch yourself and others for these symptoms: uncontrollable fits of shivering; vague, slow, slurred speech; memory lapses; incoherence; immobile, fumbling hands; frequent stumbling or a lurching gait; drowsiness (to sleep is to die); apparent exhaustion; and inability to get up after a rest.

If a member of your party develops hypothermia, he or she may deny the problem. Believe the symptoms, not the victim. Even mild symptoms demand treatment:

- Get the victim out of the wind and rain.
- Strip off all wet clothes.
- If the victim is only mildly impaired, give him or her warm drinks. Get the victim into warm clothes and a warm sleeping bag. Place well-wrapped water bottles filled with heated water close to the victim.
- If the victim is badly impaired, attempt to keep him or her awake. Put the victim in a sleeping bag with another person—both naked. If you have a double bag, put two warm people in with the victim.

To defend against hypothermia, stay dry. When clothes get wet, they lose about 90 percent of their insulating value. Wool loses relatively less heat; cotton, down, and some synthetics lose more. Choose rain clothes that cover the head, neck, body, and legs and provide good protection against wind-driven rain. Most hypothermia cases develop in air temperatures between 30 and 50 degrees F, but hypothermia can develop even in warmer temperatures.

Cora Lakes

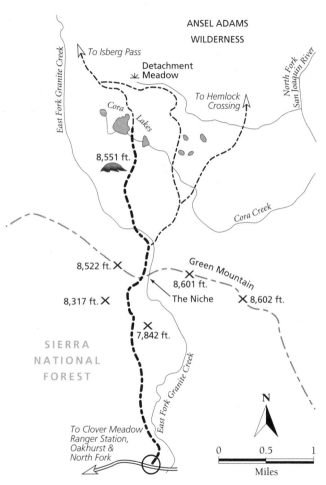

ANSEL ADAMS
WILDERNESS

To Isberg Pass

Detachment
Meadow

East Fork Granite Creek

North Fork San Joaquin River

Cora Lakes

To Hemlock
Crossing

8,551 ft.

Cora Creek

8,522 ft. ✕

Green Mountain

8,601 ft. ✕

The Niche

✕ 8,602 ft.

8,317 ft. ✕

✕
7,842 ft.

SIERRA
NATIONAL
FOREST

East Fork Granite Creek

To Clover Meadow
Ranger Station,
Oakhurst &
North Fork

N

0   0.5   1

Miles

1
CORA LAKES

Highlights: This half-day hike visits one of the dozens of lake basins in the broad Granite Creek drainage, which is immediately south of Yosemite National Park. The trail tours subalpine forests, features far-ranging vistas, and leads to a pleasant, forested lake basin.

General location: On the west side of the Sierra Nevada, in the Ansel Adams Wilderness and Sierra National Forest; 30 miles northeast of Oakhurst.

Type of hike: Round trip.

Total distance: 7.6 miles.

Elevation gain: 1,400 feet.

Best months: July through September.

Maps: Sierra National Forest map; Ansel Adams Wilderness topographic map; USGS Timber Knob.

Finding the trailhead: There are 2 ways to reach the trailhead—from the town of North Fork, or from Bass Lake.

To reach North Fork, drive north from Fresno for 28.5 miles via California 41, then turn right (east) where a sign points to "Road 200, O'Neals, North Fork, National Forest Scenic Byway." Follow this road for about 17 miles to North Fork, then turn right where a sign points to South Fork and Mammoth Pool. Stay right just past the sawmill in South Fork where a sign points to Rock Creek and Mammoth Pool. Drive the two-lane paved Forest Road 81 (the Sierra Vista Scenic Byway) into the western Sierra, following signs for Mammoth Pool and Clover Meadow.

After driving 35.8 miles from South Fork, stay left on Forest Road 81 (Sierra Vista Scenic Byway) where a right-branching road descends to Mammoth Pool Reservoir; a sign here points left to Minarets Station. Continue on this good paved road, eventually passing the Minarets Work Center on your left.

After driving 13.8 miles from the Mammoth Pool turnoff, you will reach a three-way junction. A sign here points left to Forest Road 7, Minarets Pack Station, and Beasore Meadows. Turn right at this junction onto Forest Road 5S30, and drive 1.8 miles to the Clover Meadow Ranger Station, where information is available.

From the north shore of Bass Lake, turn north onto Beasore Road (Forest Road 7), and follow signs pointing to Beasore Meadows and Clover Meadow. Forest Road 7 is a narrow, winding, steadily ascending paved road, with signs to Clover Meadow at junctions along the way. Just before reaching the turnoff to Upper Chiquito Campground, the road narrows to one lane, and its surface becomes very rough, with broken pavement and potholes. At the junction with southbound Forest Road 81, 30 miles from Bass Lake, continue straight ahead (east) on Forest Road 5S30 for 1.8 miles to Clover Meadow Ranger Station.

Continue straight past the ranger station for 0.5 mile to a junction with a road signed for Isberg Trail and Mammoth Trail. Turn left (northwest) onto Forest Road

5S30, and follow this road for 1.2 miles to a junction alongside the West Fork Granite Creek. Turn right (east) toward the Isberg Trail, staying on Forest Road 5S30. Follow this graded dirt road for another 1.3 miles to the signed Isberg Trailhead, then continue for 200 yards to the parking area on the south side of the road.

Key points:
0.0 Isberg Trailhead.
2.1 Reach the Niche.
2.4 Arrive at the junction with the trail that leads northeast to Hemlock Crossing; bear left (northwest).
2.7 Cross East Fork Granite Creek.
3.8 Arrive at Middle Cora Lake.

The hike: From the parking area, stroll west back down the road to the signed Isberg Trail, and turn right (north) onto the wide and dusty single track. The trail rises gently at first through a forest of Jeffrey pine and red fir, briefly traversing above the East Fork Granite Creek. Beyond the creek, the trail angles uphill, rising at a moderate grade and passing through viewless forest. At length the trail breaks out of the forest onto steep, open granite slopes studded with Jeffrey pine and Sierra juniper.

Vistas from this rocky, northeast-bound traverse are far ranging. Look out across the densely forested west slopes of the Sierra to the high peaks of the Silver Divide to the southeast, Kaiser Ridge to the south, and to the ice-chiseled alpine crags stretching away to the horizon.

At 2.1 miles, the traverse leads you into the Niche, a narrow gap in a high granite ridge carved by the East Fork Granite Creek. Here you enter the Ansel Adams Wilderness. Beyond the Niche, a pleasant stroll along the East Fork through open lodgepole and western white pine forest leads 0.3 mile northeast to the junction with trails that lead left (northwest) to Cora Lakes, Isberg Pass, and Yosemite National Park, and right (northeast) to Hemlock Crossing and the North Fork San Joaquin River.

Turn left (northeast), rising almost imperceptibly along the banks of the East Fork Granite Creek for 0.3 mile to a creek crossing. Anglers may be tempted to try these waters, which can produce pan-sized rainbow and brown trout. Beyond the crossing, the trail rises moderately as you ascend a forested draw. The grade levels off as the trail skirts the base of Point 8,551, a broad granite dome. Soon thereafter, at 3.8 miles, you reach the east shore and outlet of Middle Cora Lake, which at about 15 acres is the largest of the trio of lakes in this area. The lake, fringed by meadow and forest, affords a peaceful terminus to the hike. Views are limited by the pine and fir forest, though you can see the bare granite shoulders of Point 8,551 to the south. The lake contains larger fish than does Granite Creek's East Fork, but fishing is less productive in the lake as a result of steady fishing pressure throughout the summer season.

2
DUCK PASS TRAILHEAD TO ARROWHEAD LAKE

Highlights: This short hike leads from the famous road- and campground-encircled Mammoth Lakes into the glacier-carved valley of upper Mammoth Creek in the John Muir Wilderness. Six timberline tarns lie beneath the Mammoth Crest, and this trail leads to the first in that chain of scenic lakes.

General location: On the east side of the Sierra Nevada in the John Muir Wilderness and Inyo National Forest; 5 miles south of Mammoth Lakes.

Type of hike: Round trip.

Total distance: 1.8 miles.

Elevation gain: 550 feet.

Best months: July through mid-October.

Maps: Inyo National Forest map; John Muir Wilderness and Sequoia-Kings Canyon Wilderness topographic map (2 sheets); USGS Bloody Mountain.

Finding the trailhead: From Mammoth Junction on U.S. Highway 395, about 40 miles north of Bishop and 26 miles south of Lee Vining, turn west onto California 203. About 4.5 miles west of US 395, turn left (south) at the junction with the northbound Devils Postpile Road, which leads to Devils Postpile and the ski area. Follow this paved road for 5 miles to the upper end of Lake Mary,

Duck Pass Trailhead to Arrowhead Lake

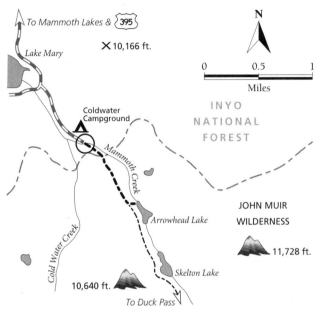

where a sign marks the entrance to Coldwater Campground. Drive 0.8 mile through the campground to the large trailhead parking area at the road's end.

Key points:

0.0 Duck Pass Trailhead.
0.8 Reach the junction with the spur trail leading left (east) to Arrowhead Lake.
0.9 Arrive at Arrowhead Lake.

The hike: Your dusty trail goes south from the huge trailhead parking area, ascending briefly along turbulent Mammoth Creek before heading into the lodgepole pine and mountain hemlock forest. The trail then ascends a steep course away from the creek, gaining 400 feet of elevation in the next 0.4 mile. The trail levels off on a forested bench in the lower reaches of the glacier-carved valley overlooking Arrowhead Lake, where you meet a signed trail leading left (east) down to the shores of that lake at 0.8 mile.

Follow the spur trail downhill for 0.1 mile to the shoreline of the aptly named lake, the lowest in a chain of 6 lakes in the upper Mammoth Creek drainage. Although fishing in the lake is poor, fine views of 11,000-foot mountains, the sound of rushing waters, and the beautiful lake combine to make this a fine place to wile away an afternoon.

Rock Creek to Long Lake
Rock Creek to Ruby Lake

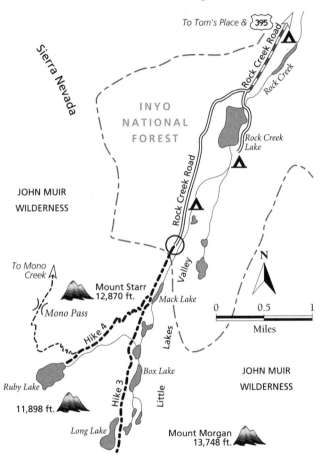

To Tom's Place & 395

Sierra Nevada

Rock Creek Road

Rock Creek

INYO
NATIONAL
FOREST

Rock Creek
Lake

JOHN MUIR
WILDERNESS

Rock Creek Road

Valley

N

To Mono
Creek

Mount Starr
12,870 ft.

Mack Lake

Mono Pass

Hike 4

0   0.5   1
Miles

Lakes

Ruby Lake

Box Lake

Hike 3

Little

JOHN MUIR
WILDERNESS

11,898 ft.

Long Lake

Mount Morgan
13,748 ft.

3
ROCK CREEK TO LONG LAKE

Highlights: This short but memorable hike begins at the highest trailhead in the Sierra, passing 5 timberline lakes brimming with hungry trout and set beneath 13,000-foot crags.

General location: On the east side of the Sierra Nevada in the John Muir Wilderness and Inyo National Forest; 20 miles northwest of Bishop.

Type of hike: Round trip.

Total distance: 4 miles.

Elevation gain: 300 feet.

Best months: July through mid-October.

Maps: Inyo National Forest map; John Muir Wilderness and Sequoia-Kings Canyon Wilderness topographic map (2 sheets); USGS Mount Morgan and Mount Abbot.

Finding the trailhead: From Tom's Place on U.S. Highway 395, 24 miles north of Bishop and 15 miles south of Mammoth Junction, turn south onto Rock Creek Road. A sign indicates Rock Creek Lake. Follow this paved road for 11 miles to the trailhead, which is at the end of the road. The final 2 miles of the road beyond Rock Creek Lake are paved but narrow, so drive with caution.

Key points:
0.0 Little Lakes Valley Trailhead.
0.6 Reach the junction with the Mono Pass Trail; stay left (south).
2.0 Arrive at Long Lake.

The hike: The hike through Little Lakes Valley follows an old double track that once was the primary access to the Pine Creek tungsten mines. It makes an excellent day hike, especially for people staying at one of the campgrounds on Rock Creek, and for those who are interested in a chance to stretch their legs and do some backcountry fishing.

From the trailhead, hike south on the old double track, skirting the west shores of long and narrow Mack Lake, and passing the trail to Mono Pass, which branches to the right (west). The jagged, snow-streaked Sierra crest peaks loom boldly at the head of the valley. Beyond the Mono Pass Trail junction at 0.6 mile, your route passes a trio of beautiful subalpine lakes surrounded by timberline stands of lodgepole and whitebark pine, each featuring good fishing and a breathtaking, high-mountain setting.

As you approach the head of the valley at 2 miles, you reach Long Lake at 10,543 feet. This is the last lake in the Little Lakes Valley chain before the trail starts climbing steadily. Chickenfoot Lake, 0.7 mile ahead, lies more than 200 feet above Long Lake.

At Long Lake, among timberline groves of lodgepole and whitebark pine, hikers will enjoy fair fishing and excellent vistas of the bold summits of Mounts Mills and Dade, and Bear Creek Spire, all rising well above 13,000 feet.

4
ROCK CREEK TO RUBY LAKE

see map page 18

Highlights: This short hike leads hikers out of lake-rich Little Lakes Valley to a hanging cirque, where beautiful Ruby Lake spreads out below the 13,000-foot crests of the Sierra.

General location: On the east side of the Sierra Nevada in the John Muir Wilderness and Inyo National Forest; 20 miles northwest of Bishop.

Type of hike: Round trip.

Total distance: 4.2 miles.

Elevation gain: 850 feet.

Best months: July through mid-October.

Maps: Inyo or Sierra National Forest maps; John Muir Wilderness and Sequoia-Kings Canyon Wilderness topographic map (2 sheets); USGS Mount Morgan and Mount Abbot.

Finding the trailhead: From Tom's Place on U.S. Highway 395, 24 miles north of Bishop and 15 miles south of Mammoth Junction, turn south onto Rock Creek Road. A sign indicates Rock Creek Lake. Follow this paved road for 11 miles to the trailhead, which is at the end of the road. The final 2 miles of the road beyond Rock Creek Lake are paved but narrow, so drive with caution.

Key points:
0.0 Little Lakes Valley Trailhead.
0.6 At the junction with Mono Pass Trail, turn right (southwest) and begin ascending.
1.9 Arrive at the junction with the spur trail to Ruby Lake; bear left (southwest).
2.1 Reach the lake shore.

The hike: The trail begins at the south end of the large parking area. The first 0.6 mile follows the route of the Rock Creek to Long Lake hike (Hike 3), passing through Little Lakes Valley in an open timberline forest of scattered lodgepole and whitebark pine. At the Mono Pass Trail junction at 0.6 mile, turn right and ascend southwest past several small benches.

After climbing for 1.3 miles, you reach the southwest-branching trail to Ruby Lake, where you turn left and gradually ascend along the lake's outlet creek. At 2.1 miles, you will reach the shores of the deep, blue, oval lake at 11,100 feet. Backed by 13,000-foot Sierra crest peaks and the broken granite headwall of the lake's cirque, rising nearly 2,000 feet from the lakeshore, this timberline gem is an attractive destination. Fishing for small rainbow and brook trout, however, is only fair.

5
NORTH LAKE TO GRASS LAKE

Highlights: Grass Lake, one of innumerable lakes in the vast Bishop Creek drainage, is the easiest backcountry lake in the area reached by trail; the hike involves only a small investment of time and energy. Unlike many Bishop Creek lakes, this grass- and forest-rimmed lake receives a comparatively light amount of day-hiking traffic.

General location: On the east side of the Sierra Nevada in the John Muir Wilderness and Inyo National Forest; 16 miles southwest of Bishop.

Type of hike: Round trip.

Total distance: 3 miles.

Elevation gain: 600 feet.

Best months: July through early October.

Maps: Inyo National Forest map; John Muir Wilderness and Sequoia-Kings Canyon Wilderness topographic map (two sheets); USGS Mount Darwin.

Finding the trailhead: From U.S. Highway 395 in Bishop, turn west onto California 168 where a sign lists mileages to South Lake, Lake Sabrina, and North Lake. Follow this paved road up Bishop Creek Canyon. After 14 miles, avoid the left-branching road to South Lake, and continue straight for 3 miles to the signed North Lake Road, which leads right (west). Follow this dirt road for 1.75 miles to the hiker's parking area just above (west of) North Lake.

North Lake to Grass Lake
Lake Sabrina to Blue Lake

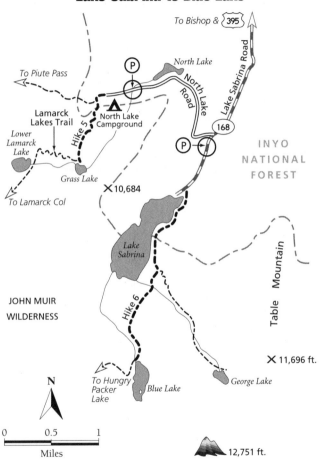

To Bishop & 395

North Lake

To Piute Pass

Lamarck Lakes Trail

North Lake Road

Lake Sabrina Road

P

North Lake Campground

168

Lower Lamarck Lake

INYO

NATIONAL

FOREST

Grass Lake

To Lamarck Col

✕ 10,684

Lake Sabrina

JOHN MUIR WILDERNESS

Hike 5

Hike 6

Table Mountain

✕ 11,696 ft.

N

To Hungry Packer Lake

Blue Lake

George Lake

0   0.5   1
Miles

▲ 12,751 ft.

Key points:
0.0 From the North Lake hiker's parking area, return to North Lake Road and walk southwest to the trailhead at the road's end.
0.5 Turn left (south) just beyond the road's end onto the Lamarck Lakes Trail.
1.5 Arrive at the junction with the Grass Lake Trail; turn left (south), and arrive at Grass Lake within a few hundred yards.

The hike: From the trailhead parking area, return to the North Lake Road and walk southwest for 0.5 mile to the trailhead. Almost immediately, you will meet the Lamarck Lakes Trail and turn left (south) on this route. You quickly begin climbing switchbacks up northwest-facing slopes clothed in aspen and lodgepole pine. Midway up the trail, you will have good views into the classic U-shaped canyon of North Fork Bishop Creek.

After climbing for 1 mile, take the short lateral trail to Grass Lake that departs to the left (south), and leads to the pleasant lodgepole-shaded and grass-fringed lake. Fishing for pan-sized trout is usually good here.

6
LAKE SABRINA TO BLUE LAKE

see map page 24

Highlights: This short but rigorous day hike leads into a spectacular, peak-rimmed alpine lake basin in the eastern Sierra.

General location: On the east side of the Sierra Nevada in the John Muir Wilderness and Inyo National Forest; 12 miles southwest of Bishop.

Type of hike: Round trip.

Total distance: 5.8 miles.

Elevation gain: 1,338 feet.

Best months: July through early October.

Maps: Inyo National Forest map; John Muir Wilderness and Sequoia-Kings Canyon Wilderness topographic map (2 sheets); USGS Mount Thompson and Mount Darwin.

Finding the trailhead: From U.S. Highway 395 in Bishop, turn west onto California 168; a sign indicates South Lake, North Lake, and Lake Sabrina. Follow this paved road up the canyon of Bishop Creek and into the Inyo National Forest. Stay right (south) at 14 miles, where the road to South Lake forks left. Drive 3 more miles to the signed Sabrina Basin hiker's parking area at the junction with the westbound North Lake Road.

Key points:

0.0 Begin at the Lake Sabrina hiker's parking area.

0.6 Reach the trailhead.

1.8 At the junction with the George Lake Trail, stay right (southwest).

2.9 Reach the outlet of Blue Lake.

The hike: The immense, glacier-carved bowl of the Middle Fork Bishop Creek, popularly known as Sabrina Basin, boasts three dozen lakes, ranging in elevation from 9,700 to 12,400 feet. Many of these lakes feature excellent fishing, and all have a backdrop of jagged crags approaching 14,000 feet. The lower lakes are typically forest-rimmed, while the higher lakes are rockbound.

Begin this hike by walking south from the hiker's parking area on Lake Sabrina Road. The jagged, snowy peaks of the Sierra crest, piercing the sky to the south, should divert your attention from this short section of pavement, giving you an exhilarating taste of what lies ahead. Leave the road after 0.6 mile, turning left (south) at the signed trailhead.

The trail traverses mostly open slopes above the east shore of Lake Sabrina. These slopes are clothed in sagebrush, mountain mahogany, scattered aspen, lodgepole and limber pine, and an occasional Sierra juniper, which is unmistakable with its shaggy, reddish bark. At 1.8 miles, the eastbound trail leading to George Lake, Table Mountain, and the Tyee Lakes leaves the route and takes off to the left.

Bearing right and continuing south at this junction, the trail crosses the outlet creek of George Lake, then crosses another small creek before beginning a series of switchbacks under the moderate shade of lodgepole pines. At 2.9 miles (about 1.1 miles past the George Lake Trail), you reach beautiful Blue Lake at 10,398 feet. The view up the canyon across the lake is outstanding. The sparsely timbered talus slopes of Thompson Ridge rise well above the 12,000-foot level east of the lake, and bold crags rise at the basin's head to the south.

The trail crosses the wide outlet of Blue Lake via a log-jam and continues up the broad basin, visiting more than one half-dozen lakes, most of which are beyond the reach of most day hikers.

7
SOUTH LAKE TO LONG LAKE

Highlights: This scenic trip ascends the dramatic South Fork Bishop Creek, surveying a landscape dominated by giant granite crags, ice-sculpted bedrock, alpine wildflower gardens, and timberline groves of whitebark pine.

General location: On the east side of the Sierra Nevada in the John Muir Wilderness and Inyo National Forest; 12 miles southwest of Bishop.

Type of hike: Round trip.

Total distance: 4.8 miles.

Elevation gain: 900 feet.

Best months: Mid-July through early October.

Maps: Inyo National Forest map; John Muir Wilderness and Sequoia-Kings Canyon Wilderness topographic map (2 sheets); USGS Mount Thompson.

Finding the trailhead: From U.S. Highway 395 in Bishop, turn west onto California 168 (Lake Sabrina Road); a sign indicates South Lake, North Lake, and Lake Sabrina. Follow this paved road up the canyon of Bishop Creek and into the Inyo National Forest. At the Lake Sabrina/South Lake junction at the 14-mile mark, turn left (east) and drive 7.5 miles to the trailhead parking area above South Lake.

Key points:

0.0 Bishop Pass Trailhead parking area.

South Lake to Long Lake

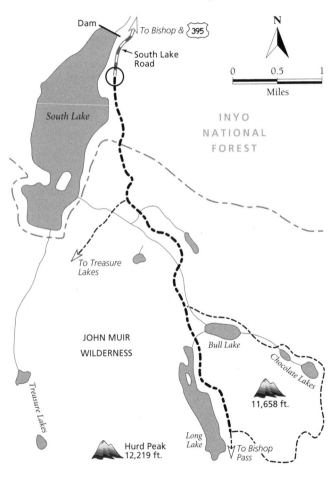

Dam

To Bishop & 395

South Lake Road

South Lake

INYO NATIONAL FOREST

N

0   0.5   1

Miles

To Treasure Lakes

JOHN MUIR WILDERNESS

Bull Lake

Chocolate Lakes

11,658 ft.

Treasure Lakes

Hurd Peak 12,219 ft.

Long Lake

To Bishop Pass

1.0 The Treasure Lakes Trail branches right (southwest); stay left (southeast).
2.0 At the junction with the trail to Bull and Chocolate Lakes, bear right (south).
2.4 Reach Long Lake.

The hike: The headwaters of the Bishop Creek drainage, spread over some 50 square miles, contain more high lakes than any other drainage on the eastern side of the Sierra. More than 80 sizable lakes, and innumerable smaller tarns, dot the many cirques in the forks of Bishop Creek.

This memorable trip ascends the basin of the South Fork Bishop Creek to a beautiful timberline lake wedged between the alpine domes of Hurd and Chocolate Peaks.

From the trailhead at the road's end, follow the well-worn and rocky trail that leads generally southeast, rising at a moderate grade over slopes studded with aspens and lodgepole pines. Good views stretch across the deep waters of South Lake to the bold Sierra crest summits of Mounts Johnson, Gilbert, and Thompson. The lower pyramidal summit of Hurd Peak guards the entrance to the alpine heights of the upper South Fork two miles to the south, and rises above Long Lake, your destination.

The trail levels off on a bench high above South Lake. At 10,250 feet, 1 mile from the trailhead, the Treasure Lakes Trail branches right (southwest). To continue to Long Lake, bear left (southeast), and ascend steadily through increasingly rocky, ice-gouged terrain studded with lodgepole and whitebark pine. Cross the South Fork along the way, and continue to the eastbound trail leading to Bull and Chocolate Lakes at 2 miles. That trail carves a 2.2-mile semicircle around those lakes and Ruwau Lake before returning to the main trail above the shores of Long Lake.

After bearing right (south) at the junction with the route to Bull and Chocolate Lakes, you will cross Long Lake's outlet stream, then begin a traverse above its eastern shore. This lovely lake, with rock- and meadow-fringed shores, offers one of the best day-hike destinations in the South Fork basin. Find a rocky knoll or a shady timberline grove along the lakeshore at 2.4 miles, and enjoy the views of bold Sierra crags before backtracking to the trailhead.

8
NORTH FORK BIG PINE CREEK TO CIENEGA MIRTH

Highlights: This memorable trip leads into one of the most majestic east-side canyons in the Sierra Nevada. Hiking to features such as the Big Pine Lakes and Palisade Glacier is beyond the reach of most day hikers, yet taking the trip as far as Cienega Mirth flats affords fine vistas of the towering peaks at the head of the canyon.

General location: On the east side of the Sierra Nevada in the John Muir Wilderness and Inyo National Forest; 8 miles west of Big Pine.

Type of hike: Round trip.

Total distance: 4.6 miles.

Elevation gain: 1,000 feet.

Best months: July through mid-October.

Maps: Inyo National Forest map; John Muir Wilderness and Sequoia-Kings Canyon Wilderness topographic map (2 sheets); USGS Coyote Flat.

Finding the trailhead: From U.S. Highway 395 in Big Pine, turn west onto Crocker Street; a sign indicates "Big Pine Recreation Area–9." Follow this paved road into the eastern Sierra for 10 miles to the signed hiker's parking area, about 0.5 mile below (east of) Glacier Lodge.

33

North Fork Big Pine Creek to Cienega Mirth

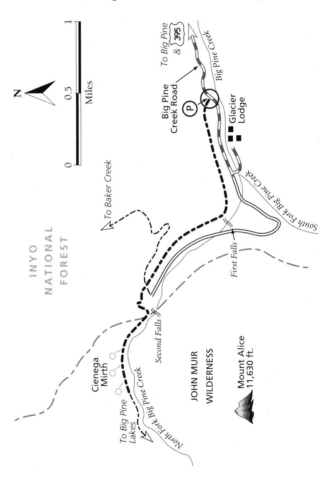

Key points:

0.0 Start at the Big Pine Creek Trailhead east of Glacier Lodge.

1.6 Continue straight (west) at the junction with the unmaintained Baker Creek Trail and the old trail descending into Big Pine Creek.

2.3 Arrive at Cienega Mirth.

The hike: The trail begins at the western edge of the parking area where a sign indicates the North Fork Trail. The trail heads west over a low hill, passes just above the pack station, then begins a moderately ascending traverse along a south-facing slope covered with sagebrush, bitterbrush, rabbitbrush, and scattered Jeffrey pines.

Over-the-shoulder views are excellent, especially those of the U-shaped canyon of Big Pine Creek framing the Inyo Mountains on the eastern horizon. Immediately across the canyon to your south, 11,896-foot Kid Mountain skyrockets more than 4,000 feet directly above Glacier Lodge. In the southwest, your view includes the Middle Palisade Glacier, the Palisade Crest, and 14,040-foot Middle Palisade, soaring above the head of the South Fork Big Pine Creek.

After hiking less than 1 mile, the trail bends northwest and passes above roaring First Falls. You will reach a junction after strolling 1.6 miles from the trailhead; the right-hand or northeast-branching trail climbs steeply over the ridge into Baker Creek, and is seldom used. The left (northwest) trail descends for 0.3 mile to the end of an old, closed road that is visible directly below.

Continue straight (northwest) toward cascading Second Falls, and after a few short switchbacks you enter the John Muir Wilderness. The trail parallels the noisy North Fork above the falls, and lodgepole pines begin mixing into the Jeffrey pine forest.

You enter the aspen-shaded Cienega Mirth area at 8,700 feet and 2.3 miles, where the brush begins to give way to grassy areas scattered with boulders and wildflowers and watered by springs emanating from the south-facing slopes to the north.

Cienega Mirth flats makes a fine destination for a half-day hike. From its boulder-studded expanse, fine views framed by lodgepole pine and aspen reach southward to 11,630-foot Mount Alice, and extend up the canyon to one of the Sierra Nevada's preeminent peaks— 12,999-foot Temple Crag.

9
TWIN LAKES

Highlights: This short hike, which leads to a subalpine lake basin on the western slopes of the Sierra, features ice-sculpted landscapes, cool forests, vigorous streams, and good trout fishing.

General location: On the west side of the Sierra Nevada in the Kaiser Wilderness and Sierra National Forest; 55 miles northeast of Fresno.

Type of hike: Round trip.

Total distance: 5.8 miles.

Elevation gain: 500 feet.

Best months: Mid-July through October.

Maps: Sierra National Forest map; Kaiser Wilderness topographic map; USGS Kaiser Peak.

Finding the trailhead: From Fresno, follow California 168 northeast for 71 miles into the Sierra, pass through the town of Shaver Lake, and continue to the east end of Huntington Lake. At the signed junction, turn right (northeast) onto the paved, two-lane Kaiser Pass Road (Forest Road 80), which leads to Mono Hot Springs, Lake Edison, and Florence Lake.

This steadily ascending road becomes a narrow, winding, and steep single lane of pavement after 6.7 miles; drive with extreme caution. The road tops out on 9,160-foot Kaiser Pass after 7.4 miles, then descends for 2.1

Twin Lakes

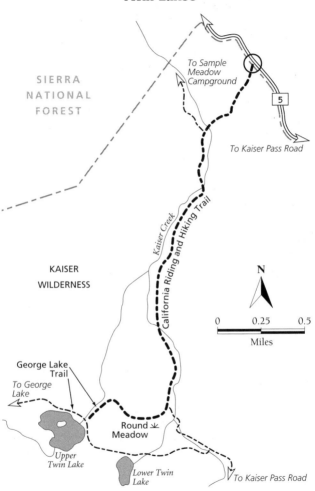

SIERRA
NATIONAL
FOREST

5

To Sample
Meadow
Campground

To Kaiser Pass Road

Kaiser Creek

California Riding and Hiking Trail

KAISER
WILDERNESS

N

0   0.25   0.5
Miles

George Lake
Trail

To George
Lake

Round
Meadow

Upper
Twin Lake

Lower Twin
Lake

To Kaiser Pass Road

miles to the junction with Forest Road 5, signed for Sample Meadow Campground. Turn left (west) and follow this good gravel road for 2.2 miles to the spacious California Riding and Hiking Trailhead parking area, which is on the east side of the road. There is space for 15 to 20 vehicles, and an information signboard is located on the west side of the road where the trail begins.

Key points:
0.0 California Riding and Hiking Trailhead.
0.5 Bear left (south) at the junction with Kaiser Creek Trail.
1.9 Cross the Round Meadow branch of Kaiser Creek.
2.3 At the junction with George Lake Trail, turn right (southwest).
2.9 Arrive at Upper Twin Lake.

The hike: Kaiser Ridge is a major east-west divide rising north of Huntington Lake on the west slope of the Sierra. Much of this broken, 10,000-foot ridge is protected within the boundaries of the 22,700-acre Kaiser Wilderness, an isolated island of high country rising far west of the High Sierra. This easily accessible wilderness area contains two dozen high lakes, alpine crests featuring far-ranging vistas, and enough backcountry trails to satisfy both day hikers and long-distance backpackers alike.

The subalpine Twin Lakes basin is one of the most scenic spots in the Kaiser Wilderness, set beneath the splintered granite crest of Kaiser Ridge. Unless you like lots of company, avoid this hike on holiday weekends.

With 3 trails leading to Upper Twin Lake, the basin is at times downright overcrowded.

The California Riding and Hiking Trail begins behind the information signboard on the west side of Forest Road 5, and winds on the level along the edge of selectively logged forest, staying inside an uncut forest of lodgepole pine, and red and white fir. After a few hundred yards you enter the Kaiser Wilderness at a Sierra National Forest sign, and then begin to gradually descend along the sometimes rocky trail. Lodgepole pine dominates the forest, along with boulder-dotted grassy openings that host sagebrush, aspen, currant, and wildflowers such as aster, yarrow, mule-ears, groundsel, and cinquefoil.

The descent ends when you reach the alder-lined banks of Kaiser Creek; turn left (south) and follow the east bank of the creek briefly upstream. Quite soon the trail appears to end; at this point you should make a hard right turn and cross the large logs spanning the creek. The stock ford lies a few yards downstream from the log crossing. Just a few yards beyond the crossing at the 0.5-mile mark, you probably will not notice the seldom-used Kaiser Creek Trail joining the trail from the right (north).

Cross back to the east bank of Kaiser Creek at another log/stock ford crossing, then resume the pleasant, gradual uphill walk through the pine and fir forest. An understory of green shrubs and the verdant foliage of myriad wildflowers is unusually rich in this shady forest.

At 1.9 miles, you will rock-hop the Round Meadow branch of Kaiser Creek. Beyond the crossing, the trail ascends a steady, moderate to sometimes steep grade, rising through an increasingly rockbound landscape with extensive areas of bare granite and glacier-deposited boulders (erratics). Red fir and western white pine become the dominant forest trees during this ascent.

At 2.3 miles and 8,480 feet, you reach a junction on a sagebrush-clad slope. The left fork, which loops back to this junction from Upper Twin Lake, is signed for Badger Flat. Turn right (southwest) onto the trail signed for Twin Lakes (the George Lake Trail). The trail quickly tops a rise and turns west, traversing open slopes studded with lodgepole pine and aspen above the verdant spread of Round Meadow. You will enjoy splendid views of the broken north faces and tree-feathered crests of Kaiser Ridge as you hike. This traverse soon curves northwest and crests a minor saddle set beneath a broken slope of metamorphic rocks.

Beyond the saddle, you come to another small creek and once again cross its course via logs. On the west bank of that stream, turn left (south), and after a brief ascent, stroll down to the northeast shore of the lovely, trout-filled waters of Upper Twin Lake at 2.9 miles.

Broken, ice-chiseled granite rises behind the lake to the tree-studded Kaiser Ridge, and a bold array of cliffs and 10,000-foot peaks rise immediately west and southwest of the lake. Ice-polished granite slopes and a scattering of red fir, western white pine, and lodgepole pine add to the beauty of the basin, which lies in a lovely subalpine setting—a miniature version of the High Sierra. Fishing for abundant pan-sized trout is often excellent here.

10
COURTRIGHT RESERVOIR TO CLIFF LAKE

Highlights: This trip leads hikers into an "island" of high country on the western slopes of the Sierra, where dense conifer forests and rich meadows merge with a rocky crest of 10,000-foot peaks.

General location: On the west side of the Sierra Nevada in the Dinkey Lakes Wilderness and Sierra National Forest; 50 miles northeast of Fresno.

Type of hike: Round trip.

Total distance: 10 miles.

Elevation gain: 1,025 feet.

Best months: July through mid-October.

Maps: Sierra National Forest map; Dinkey Lakes Wilderness topographic map; USGS Courtright Reservoir, Dogtooth Peak, and Nelson Mountain.

Finding the trailhead: From Clovis, proceed northeast on California 168 for about 40 miles to the community of Shaver Lake. Turn right (east) near the southern end of Shaver Lake; a sign indicates Dinkey Creek and Wishon Dam lie ahead. Follow the paved Dinkey Creek Road generally eastward for 11.6 miles to a junction just south of Dinkey Creek.

Turn right (east) just beyond the pack station onto McKinley Grove Road (Forest Road 40), where the sign

Courtright Reservoir to Cliff Lake

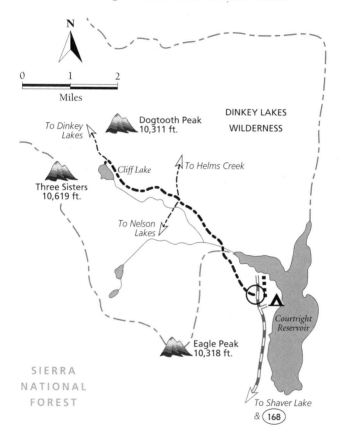

N

| 0 | 1 | 2 |

Miles

DINKEY LAKES
WILDERNESS

Dogtooth Peak
10,311 ft.

*To Dinkey
Lakes*

Cliff Lake

To Helms Creek

Three Sisters
10,619 ft.

*To Nelson
Lakes*

*Courtright
Reservoir*

Eagle Peak
10,318 ft.

SIERRA
NATIONAL
FOREST

To Shaver Lake
& 168

43

directs you toward McKinley Grove, Wishon Reservoir, and Courtright Reservoir. Follow this paved road southeast for 13.6 miles, passing through the McKinley Grove of giant sequoias, to a junction with the right-branching road to Wishon Reservoir. Turn left (northwest) here onto Forest Road 10S16), following the good paved road toward Courtright Village (no services), and the Cliff Lake Trailhead, which is about 10 miles from the previous junction, and 35.2 miles from Shaver Lake.

Key points:

0.0 Trailhead.

3.0 Continue straight (northwest) at the junction with the trails to Helms Meadow (northeast) and Nelson Lakes (southwest).

4.9 Reach the junction with the southwest-bound spur trail to Cliff Lake. Turn left and descend to the lake.

5.0 Arrive at Cliff Lake.

The hike: From the parking area, the trail heads northwest through a red fir and lodgepole pine forest on a slightly descending grade. You will soon pass a double track joining the trail on the right (east). As you approach the northwest end of Courtright Reservoir, the forest becomes dominated by lodgepole pine. Hop across the creek draining Cliff Lake and enter the Dinkey Lakes Wilderness. This creek runs high during spring runoff, so early-season hikers may be forced to wade.

The trail meanders northwest through a heavy lodgepole pine forest, reaching a four-way junction 3 miles from the trailhead. The seldom used trail leads northeast to Helms Meadow and beyond, while the southwest trail, equally seldom trod, leads to the Nelson Lakes and beyond.

Continue straight (northwest) on the Cliff Lake Trail, noting the addition of red and white fir to the previously unvaried lodgepole pine forest. You eventually begin a moderate ascent via switchbacks along a south-facing slope clothed in western white pine and manzanita, enjoying views of Courtright Reservoir and a host of granite domes that surround it. Far to the east the alpine peaks of the LeConte Divide and other High Sierra summits form a sawtoothed skyline. A short distance to the south and southwest rise Brown Peak (10,349 feet), Nelson Mountain (10,218 feet), and Eagle Peak (10,318 feet), soaring high above their thickly forested basins.

The trail levels off above the switchbacks, and you will find yourself at an elevation of 9,500 feet as you hike above the northeast shore of beautiful Cliff Lake at 4.9 miles. Near the west end of the lake, turn left (southwest) on the descending spur trail that leads you quickly down to the upper end of the lake at 9,400 feet. With a backdrop of 400-foot-high cliffs and an open, boulder-dotted forest surrounding its shores, the lake is an excellent and worthwhile destination.

11
ROWELL TRAILHEAD TO ROWELL MEADOW

Highlights: This short trip surveys the pleasant meadow and forest country in the Jennie Lakes Wilderness, which is on the western slope of the southern Sierra Nevada, high above Kings Canyon.

General location: On the west side of the Sierra Nevada in the Jennie Lakes Wilderness and Sequoia National Forest; 60 miles east of Fresno.

Type of hike: Round trip.

Total distance: 5.2 miles.

Elevation gain: 970 feet.

Best months: July through mid-October.

Maps: Sequoia National Forest map; Jennie Lakes Wilderness and Monarch Wilderness topographic map; USGS Mount Silliman and Muir Grove.

Finding the trailhead: These directions begin from the signed Big Meadows turnoff on the Generals Highway, which connects California 180 and California 198 and is the main road through Sequoia National Park. The Big Meadows turnoff is about 63 miles east of Fresno via CA 180 and the Generals Highway, and 72.5 miles east of Visalia via CA 198 and the Generals Highway.

At the turnoff, turn east and follow paved Big Meadows Road (Forest Road 14S11) toward Big

Rowell Trailhead to Rowell Meadow

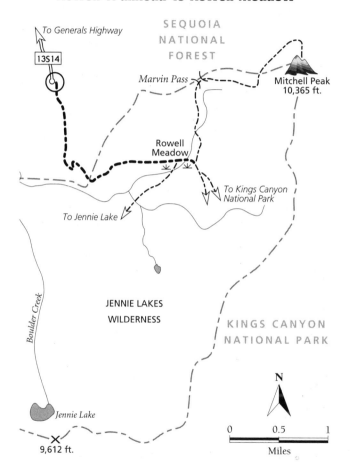

To Generals Highway

SEQUOIA
NATIONAL
FOREST

13S14

Marvin Pass

Mitchell Peak
10,365 ft.

Rowell
Meadow

To Kings Canyon
National Park

To Jennie Lake

Boulder Creek

JENNIE LAKES
WILDERNESS

KINGS CANYON
NATIONAL PARK

N

Jennie Lake

9,612 ft.

0   0.5   1

Miles

Meadows, as indicated by signs at numerous junctions. After driving 4.75 miles from the highway, bear right where an old sign indicates Kings Canyon Pack Station (a.k.a. Horse Corral Pack Station) and Horse Corral Meadow. After driving 9.1 miles from the Generals Highway, turn right (east) on Forest Road 13S14 immediately before the paved road crosses Horse Corral Creek. A sign indicates Rowell Trailhead and Horse Corral Pack Station. Follow FR 13S14, a fairly rough dirt road, generally south for 2 miles to its end at the trailhead parking area, which is high above Boulder Creek canyon.

Key points:
0.0 Rowell Trailhead.
2.4 At the junction with the Jennie Lake Trail, bear left (east).
2.6 Arrive at the three-way trail junction in Rowell Meadow.

The hike: The trail begins on the east side of the road, just north of the parking area, and heads east, ascending a moderate grade through a forest of red and white fir. It soon jogs south and begins traversing rocky and forested slopes far above Boulder Creek canyon. After hiking 1.4 miles, the trail bends northeast, traversing sunny, rockbound slopes above Gannon Creek, a noisy Boulder Creek tributary.

The trail eventually approaches a small creek and begins ascending along its course, under a canopy of lodgepole pines. Leaving the small creek behind, the trail levels off on a meadow-floored, wildflower-brightened, and lodgepole-shaded plateau, soon passing just north of the Rowell Meadow snow survey shelter. A wilderness ranger uses this cabin as a base camp during the summer season.

The trail continues east from the cabin, passing a southbound trail leading to JO Pass, Gannon Creek, and Jennie Lake at 2.4 miles. Continue eastward through the lodgepole pine forest to an easy crossing of a small creek just below a pool filled with small trout. The trail junction at 2.6 miles on the east bank of the creek marks the end of this hike.

Option: Most day hikers will be content enjoying the shady lodgepole forests and verdant spread of Rowell Meadow before backtracking to the trailhead, but strong day hikers may wish to continue north and east for an additional 2.6 miles to the summit of 10,365-foot Mitchell Peak. From the peak, you will enjoy broad vistas of the Sequoia-Kings Canyon wilderness and the west slopes of the Sierra.

12
LOOKOUT PEAK

Highlights: This short, rewarding hike leads to a panoramic vista point featuring dramatic views of Kings Canyon and the great peaks of the southern High Sierra.

General location: On the west side of the Sierra Nevada in the Sequoia National Forest; 60 miles east of Fresno.

Type of hike: Round trip.

Total distance: 1.2 miles.

Elevation gain: 531 feet.

Best months: Late June through October.

Maps: Sequoia National Forest map; Monarch Wilderness and Jennie Lakes Wilderness topographic map; USGS Cedar Grove.

Finding the trailhead: These directions begin from the signed Big Meadows turnoff on the Generals Highway, which connects California 180 and California 198 and is the main road through Sequoia National Park.

Turn east onto Big Meadows Road (Forest Road 14S11) and drive for 9.1 miles. Avoid the southbound spur road heading to Rowell Trailhead (Hike 11), and continue straight on Forest Road 14S11.

After 9.5 miles, the pavement ends at the junction with the southbound Forest Road 14S12, which leads to the Marvin Pass Trailhead. Continue straight (northeast) at that junction, stay right (northeast) at the next junction

Lookout Peak

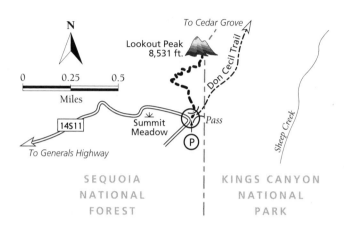

at 11.4 miles, then bear left (still northeast) at an unsigned junction with an unnamed, graded dirt road at 11.5 miles. After 13.2 miles, you approach a saddle immediately south of Lookout Peak and reach another unsigned junction. Turn left (east), and drive the final few yards to a spacious parking area on the saddle at the Don Cecil Trailhead. There is ample parking space here, and undeveloped campsites in a park-like forest of pine and fir.

Key points:
0.0 Begin at the Don Cecil Trailhead, but follow the unsigned Lookout Peak Trail north.
0.6 Arrive on Lookout Peak.

The hike: Lookout Peak, a boulder-stacked granite crag, lies just outside the Monarch Wilderness boundary on the western edge of Kings Canyon National Park. Its 8,531-foot summit stands more than 4,000 feet above Kings Canyon, one of the Sierra Nevada's most profound gorges. The short but fairly rigorous hike to the summit block rewards hikers with stunning vistas into Kings Canyon, and beyond the canyon to the lofty crags of the High Sierra.

From the saddle at the road's end, the only signed trail you will find is the Don Cecil Trail, which descends 3,500 feet in 6.5 miles to Kings Canyon near Cedar Grove. The Lookout Peak Trail, which is faint at first, leads north across the broad saddle behind the "trail" sign, toward the cone of Lookout Peak. Blazes on tall pines help show the way.

Quite soon an obvious single track appears, and you will follow this trail, gradually ascending through an open forest of ponderosa pine, and red and white fir. The grade becomes moderate, and occasionally steep, as you follow an ascending traverse along the southwest slopes of the peak. Manzanita and chinquapin are massed in clumps on the peak's steep slopes, and a park-like forest of pines and large granite boulders add to the beauty of the scene.

The trail approaches the peak's steep west ridge, then begins a series of moderately steep switchbacks ascending the south slopes. About 100 yards below the boulder-stacked summit, adjacent to one of the two low, wide radio transmitters, the trail becomes obscured among granite boulders. Acrophobic hikers are advised to end their ascent at the first radio tower, and enjoy the view into Kings Canyon from there.

Those with no fear of heights should scramble up the final 100 yards. Gaining about 50 feet, a very steep path among boulders leads to the summit blocks above the second radio tower at 0.6 mile. Find a perch and enjoy the breathtaking vista, or scramble Class 2 to Class 3 rock to the very summit.

A knife-blade granite ridge juts northeast from the summit into the abyss, pointing toward the alpine heights of Comb Ridge and the Monarch Divide, a lofty crest of 11,000-foot summits. On the northern skyline rises the landmark spire of Mount Harrington in the Monarch Wilderness, with the verdant slopes of Happy Gap notching the Monarch Divide west of that peak. The incomparable U-shaped trough of Kings Canyon, lying 4,000 feet and 2 miles below your perch, stretches eastward toward lofty crests notched with great cirques and punctuated by bold crags.

Mounts Gardiner, Cotter, and Clarence King are especially prominent on the eastern skyline. North Dome and Grand Sentinel guard the entrance to the vast Sequoia-Kings Canyon Wilderness at the road's end far below in Kings Canyon. The view also extends up the valley of Bubbs Creek, and southeast past the Roaring River drainage to the peaks of Sphinx Crest and the Great Western Divide. In the foreground, the cavernous gorge of Sheep Creek falls away at your feet, while the fir-forested north slopes of Sentinel Ridge march off toward the east.

You must eventually abandon these far-reaching vistas, and retrace your route from Lookout Peak to the trailhead.

13
BOOLE TREE LOOP TRAIL

Highlights: This scenic half-day hike features far-ranging vistas and visits the largest giant sequoia in any national forest.

General location: On the west side of the Sierra Nevada in the Sequoia National Forest; 45 miles east of Fresno.

Type of hike: Loop.

Total distance: 2.5 miles.

Elevation gain: 700 feet.

Best months: Mid-June through October.

Maps: Sequoia National Forest map; USGS Hume (part of the loop trail is not shown on the quad).

Finding the trailhead: Follow California 180 to the Big Stump Entrance to Kings Canyon National Park, about 54 miles east of Fresno. Continue for another 1.6 miles to The Wye, where you turn left (north) on CA 180 toward Grant Grove and Cedar Grove. Pass through Grant Grove Village 1.5 miles from The Wye, then proceed 4.3 miles northeast to the junction with Forest Road 13S55. This junction is signed for Converse Basin, Stump Meadow, and Boole Tree Trail.

Turn left (northwest) onto this good but narrow dirt road, and drive 0.3 mile to a four-way junction. Continue straight (west) where the sign points to the Boole Tree Trail. After 1.9 miles, bear right (north) at the signed

Boole Tree Loop Trail

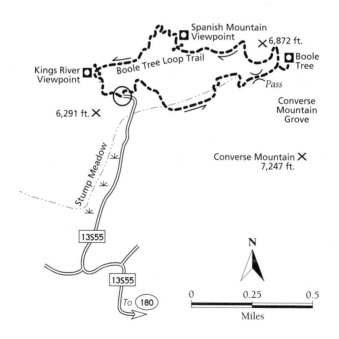

Cabin Creek Grove

SEQUOIA NATIONAL FOREST

Cabin Creek

$\times$ 6,351 ft.

Spanish Mountain Viewpoint

$\times$ 6,872 ft.

Boole Tree

Kings River Viewpoint

Boole Tree Loop Trail

Pass

Converse Mountain Grove

6,291 ft. $\times$

Converse Mountain $\times$ 7,247 ft.

Stump Meadow

13S55

13S55

To 180

N

0   0.25   0.5

Miles

junction, then dip into Stump Meadow and ascend to the spacious trailhead parking area at the road's end, 2.6 miles from CA 180. There is room for as many as 30 vehicles at the trailhead. Pit toilets and an informational signboard showing a map of the trail are also located here.

Key points:
0.0 From the trailhead, turn right (east) onto the loop trail.
1.0 Reach the Boole Tree.
1.6 Arrive at the Spanish Mountain Viewpoint.
2.3 Visit the Kings River Viewpoint.
2.5 Return to the trailhead.

The hike: Unlike many other giant sequoia trails, the Boole Tree Trail visits only one ancient giant sequoia. Until the 1890s, the sequoias of Converse Basin constituted the largest grove in existence. Today only giant stumps are left behind, along with the renewed growth of young sequoias and the Boole Tree. Standing 269 feet tall, and with a diameter of 29 feet, this tree is the largest sequoia standing outside the boundaries of California's national parks.

This 2.5-mile loop trail is immensely rewarding, passing through mixed conifer forest, including a multitude of young sequoias, en route to the Boole Tree, then returning to the trailhead via the rim of Kings Canyon, which features outstanding vistas. Although portions of the trail have a moderately steep grade, it is a short hike suitable for hikers of all ability levels.

Take the loop in a counterclockwise direction, climbing to the Boole Tree, then enjoy Kings Canyon vistas along the downhill stretch. Begin by taking the right fork of the loop trail from the trailhead, ascending a moderate grade through an open forest of ponderosa pine, incense-cedar, sugar pine, and young sequoias. The trailside slopes are mantled in a green blanket of fragrant kit-kit-dizze (a member of the rose family), clumps of manzanita, and bracken fern in shady niches.

Soon the grade steepens, leading you up a verdant draw drained by a trickling seasonal stream. Many of the willows that crowd the bottom of the draw are unusually tall, spreading, and multi-branched. White fir also joins the forest ranks within the confines of the draw. Once the grade moderates, you step across the small stream and exit the draw, heading north. The trail rises via switchbacks, then straightens out as it leads steeply, but briefly, uphill to the crest of a ridge north of Converse Mountain. On this apparently dry ridge grow thickets of mountain whitethorn and chinquapin, along with clumps of tall willows—a sure sign of moisture just below the surface.

From the ridge, the trail briefly descends the east slopes of the ridge, reenters forest, and reaches a trail sign at the junction with the Boole Tree spur trail. Turn right (south), and stroll 50 yards down to an interpretive sign explaining the history of the logging of the Converse Basin Grove in the 1890s. The Boole Tree was then thought to have been the largest giant sequoia in existence, and perhaps that is why it was the only forest monarch spared in this once vast grove.

The trail continues for about 100 yards more to the

base of the Boole Tree at 1 mile, passing second-growth sequoias along the way. This is a magnificent old tree, dead and broken at the crown, with a long, hollow fire scar on its stout bole.

From the Boole Tree, return to the loop trail, then turn right and begin a northbound ascent across open slopes. Vistas to the east are breathtaking along this stretch, reaching into the profound gorge of Kings Canyon and beyond to distant High Sierra crags. The trail levels out as it curves around the south and west slopes of a ridgetop prominence, then begins a gradual descent westward along the brushy ridge, which is studded with mixed conifers and granite boulders. Pass an old shed, then go through a gate in a fence line, and begin descending north.

The Spanish Mountain Viewpoint shown on the trail-head map is along this ridge at 1.6 miles, and the vistas are outstanding. Below you to the north is the Grand Canyon-like gorge of Kings Canyon, including a view of the churning river lying 5,000 feet far below. The Kings Canyon Special Management Area, a 49,000-acre roadless expanse adjacent to the north unit of the Monarch Wilderness, can also be seen here. You can see from the grasslands and oak woodlands of the Sierra foothills to the high alpine peaks of the Dinkey Lakes country to the north—a view that takes in the entire spectrum of western Sierra environments.

Rising high on the northeast skyline is the 10,051-foot summit of Spanish Mountain. The vertical distance between the summit of that peak and the floor of Kings

Canyon is 8,200 feet, giving this part of the canyon the distinction of being America's deepest gorge.

From this viewpoint, the trail begins a steady descent, via switchbacks, of north-facing slopes studded with ponderosa pine, white fir, willow, black oak, and young sequoias. After the long series of switchbacks ends, you regain the now lower ridge, and stroll westward along its crest. The trail eventually curves southwest and passes through another steel gate in the same fence line mentioned above. Pause just before passing through the gate and enjoy the superb vistas at the Kings River Viewpoint at 2.3 miles. Look north to the churning rapids of the Wild and Scenic Kings River.

From the gate, the trail gradually descends through fields of aromatic kit-kit-dizze for 0.2 mile to the trailhead parking area.

Horseshoe Meadow

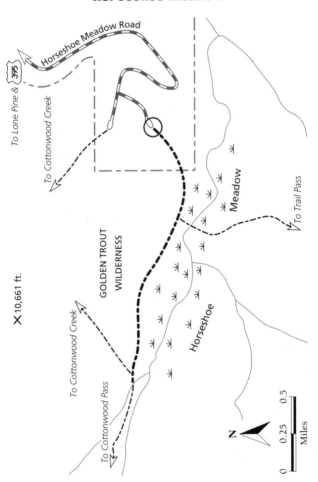

14

HORSESHOE MEADOW

Highlights: This scenic hike has no particular destination other than the spreading grasslands of 10,000-foot Horseshoe Meadow, located where the rolling landscapes of the Kern Plateau merge with the bold alpine peaks of the High Sierra.

General location: On the east side of the Sierra Nevada in the Golden Trout Wilderness and Inyo National Forest; 12 miles southwest of Lone Pine.

Type of hike: Round trip.

Total distance: 2.4 miles.

Elevation gain: 70 feet.

Best months: July through mid-October.

Maps: Inyo National Forest map; John Muir Wilderness and Sequoia-Kings Canyon Wilderness topographic map (2 sheets) or Golden Trout Wilderness and South Sierra Wilderness topographic map; USGS Cirque Peak.

Finding the trailhead: From U.S. Highway 395 in Lone Pine, turn west onto the signed Whitney Portal Road. Follow this road along Lone Pine Creek and through the boulder-covered Alabama Hills for 3.5 miles to the signed Horseshoe Meadow Road, and turn left (south). Ahead, you can see the switchbacks of the road ascending the great eastern escarpment of the Sierra Nevada. Follow this good paved road for about 19 miles to a junction. Bear left (straight) and drive 0.3 mile to the Cottonwood Pass Trailhead at the end of the road.

Key points:

0.0 Cottonwood Pass Trailhead.

0.2 Reach the junction with the southbound Trail Pass Trail; continue straight (west).

1.0 At the junction with the trail to the northeast, stay left (west).

1.2 Arrive at the west end of Horseshoe Meadow.

The hike: The long drive up the eastern escarpment of the southern Sierra via the paved Horseshoe Meadow Road is an adventure in itself. The road rises from 4,000 feet in the arid Owens Valley to the timberline forests at Horseshoe Meadow at 10,000 feet. The road's end is a popular jumping-off point for backpack trips into the John Muir and Golden Trout Wilderness Areas and the backcountry of Sequoia National Park. Consequently, most of the users of this road are either backpackers or scenic drivers. There are, numerous day-hiking destinations in the area, though few of them are easy to reach.

This short hike combines the scenic drive along the Horseshoe Meadow Road with an easy stroll along the fringes of spreading Horseshoe Meadow, a sparse grassland that is 2 miles long and up to 0.75-mile wide. There is no particular destination to the hike; simply walk as far as you wish along the level trail and enjoy the view of Sierra crest peaks from open forests of lodgepole and foxtail pines.

From the Cottonwood Pass Trailhead, follow the Cottonwood Pass Trail west for 0.2 mile to the junction with southbound Trail Pass Trail, and stay right, continuing west. The Cottonwood Pass Trail follows the northern margin of Horseshoe Meadow, staying just inside the forest of lodgepole and foxtail pines. Fine views stretch up to the rocky cone of 11,623-foot Trail Peak to the south, and reach westward to the notch of Cottonwood Pass and to Peak 12,336 immediately north of the pass.

Horseshoe Meadow is drained by several small streams that support a small population of golden trout. The meadow opening is dominated by sand and sagebrush, with only remnants of grasses and sedges along the watercourses—the results of past overgrazing.

After 1 mile, a seldom-used trail turns right (northeast) toward Cottonwood Creek. Stay left (west); 0.2 mile ahead the meadow ends and the trail enters the forest alongside a small, meadow-bordered stream. From the stream, the trail begins its steep ascent to Cottonwood Pass, and this marks the best turnaround point for an easy day hike.

15
JORDAN PEAK

Highlights: This rewarding trip leads to a lookout-capped peak on the Western Divide, where memorable vistas of the southern High Sierra unfold.

General location: On the west side of the Sierra Nevada in the Sequoia National Forest; 30 miles northeast of Porterville.

Type of hike: Round trip.

Total distance: 1.6 to 4 miles.

Elevation gain: 715 to 915 feet.

Best months: Mid-June through October.

Maps: Sequoia National Forest map; USGS Camp Nelson.

Finding the trailhead: There are two ways to locate the beginning of this remote hike—either from Porterville via tortuously twisting and turning California Highway 190, or from Kernville via the Kern River Road and the Western Divide Highway.

From Porterville, follow CA 190 east for about 40 miles to a junction with northbound Forest Road 21S50. A sign indicating that the Golden Trout Wilderness Pack Trains are 7.5 miles to the north marks this junction. There is also a highway sign at this point indicating Johnsondale, California Hot Springs, and Kernville, with mileage listings to these points. Turn left (north) here. The

Jordan Peak

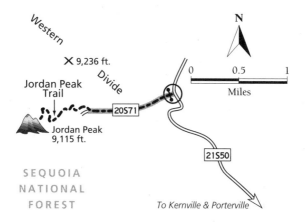

pavement ends after 4.5 miles; turn left (northwest) where a sign points to Clicks Creek Trailhead.

Continuing northwest on FR 21S50, bear right (northwest) 1.2 miles from the end of the pavement where a sign points to Clicks Creek Trailhead, Jordan Peak Lookout, and Summit Trailhead. After driving another 1.7 miles, turn left (west) where a sign points to Jordan Peak Lookout. This westbound road, Forest Road 20S71, is closed annually from November 1 through June 1. If you intend to take this hike at a leisurely pace, park here; if you are in a hurry, drive west on FR 20S71 for another 1.2 miles to the signed trailhead.

From Kernville, drive north up the Kern River on locally signed Sierra Way (Kern River Road). After driving about 19 miles along the Kern River, bear left (west) where the Sherman Pass Road branches right (east), then cross the river via a two-lane bridge.

After driving 4 miles from the river, avoid a left-branching road leading south to the abandoned lumber mill town of Johnsondale, and 0.6 mile farther, avoid a right (north) branching road leading to Camp Whitsett and beyond. Turn left (southwest) where the sign points to the Western Divide Highway. Avoid a left (southwest) branching road to Thompson Camp 8 miles from the river; this road leads to California Hot Springs.

After driving 11.2 miles from the Kern River, turn right (north) onto the Western Divide Highway; a sign here points toward California 190, Ponderosa, and Camp Nelson. Follow this good paved road north, avoiding several signed spur roads.

At a point about 15.2 miles from the Western Divide junction, and 26.5 miles from the Kern River, turn sharply right (northeast) onto FR 21S50, just beyond a sign listing mileage to Camp Nelson, Springville, and Porterville. From here, follow the instructions given in the Porterville directions to reach the trailhead.

Key points:
0.0 From the gate on Forest Road 20S71, follow the road uphill (west).
1.2 At the junction, turn right (west) onto the Jordan Peak Trail.
2.0 Arrive on Jordan Peak.

The hike: The sweeping vistas from the summit of Jordan Peak easily justify the long and scenic mountain drive to the trailhead. As you will see while atop Jordan Peak, glaciers largely did not affect the extreme southern Sierra Nevada. The landscape that meets your gaze, especially the Kern Plateau to the east, clearly illustrates the rounded, plateau-like character of the region that presented itself millions of years ago, before the Sierra Nevada batholith began uplifting to its present height. Many lofty, alpine peaks in the High Sierra also escaped glaciation, standing far above the rivers of ice, so they, too, are remnants of the broad, gentle surfaces that characterized the region in ancient times.

From the gate on FR 20S71, proceed west on the gently graded road through red fir forest. You occasionally pass logged-over openings, and the road passes over a few spring-fed creeklets. After strolling 1.2 miles, you meet the signed Jordan Peak Trail, which is on your right (west). Take the trail; the road ends at a turnout 0.1 mile beyond.

The trail leads southwest and soon begins to follow switchbacks up a slope covered with a selectively cut red fir forest. As you near the summit, chinquapin, mountain whitethorn, and manzanita begin to invade sunny openings. A few final switchbacks bring hikers to the summit at 2 miles.

Silver pines (also known as western white pines) grow on the north slope of the peak, preferring the colder microclimate that prevails there. These trees are closely related to the five-needled sugar pine, but are distinguished by smaller cones.

Upon surmounting the summit of Jordan Peak, you immediately understand why this peak was chosen as a site for a fire lookout tower—the view is truly far-reaching, and splendid as well. To the northeast, the jagged, alpine peaks of the Great Western Divide line the horizon. To the west lies the gaping chasm of the North Fork of Middle Fork Tule River, more than 5,000 feet below. Moses Mountain, at 9,331 feet, soars westward from the depths of that canyon, and 10,042-foot Maggie Mountain, with its 10,000-foot satellite summits, rises to the east.

Far to the east lies the Kern Plateau, punctuated by 12,123-foot Olancha Peak. Kern Peak also is visible on the northeastern skyline. The massive flanks of Slate Mountain, peaking at 9,302 feet, rise to the south above Camp Nelson and the South Fork of Middle Fork Tule River. On the southwest horizon, the Mount Pinos region can be seen, and on a clear day you can gaze across the broad plain of the San Joaquin Valley to the southern Coast Ranges on the western horizon.

These truly inspiring vistas will cause hikers to linger. The lookout is occupied during fire season, usually from June through October.

From the peak, retrace your route to the trailhead.

16
BLACKROCK TRAILHEAD TO CASA VIEJA MEADOWS

Highlights: This pleasant hike, which is downhill most of the way to Casa Vieja Meadows, surveys classic Kern Plateau scenery, leading through shady pine and fir forests to a rich meadow in the Golden Trout Wilderness.

General location: On the west side of the Sierra Nevada in the Golden Trout Wilderness and the Inyo National Forest; 75 miles northeast of Bakersfield.

Type of hike: Round trip.

Total distance: 4.6 miles.

Elevation loss: 600 feet.

Best months: Late June through mid-October.

Maps: Sequoia National Forest map; Golden Trout Wilderness and South Sierra Wilderness topographic map; USGS Casa Vieja Meadows.

Finding the trailhead: From Kernville, drive about 19 miles up the Kern River Road (Sierra Way), then turn right (east) onto Sherman Pass Road (Forest Road 41/22S05). This road quickly climbs eastward out of the Kern River Canyon and begins a steady ascent through the Brush Creek drainage. After 3.1 miles, pass a gate that is usually closed between late November and late May.

The road surmounts Sherman Pass 14.4 miles from the river; continue east, then north, avoiding numerous

Blackrock Trailhead to Casa Vieja Meadows

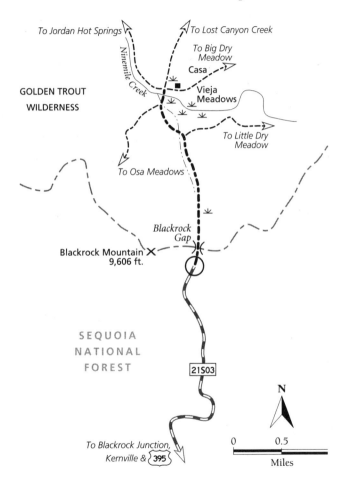

To Jordan Hot Springs

To Lost Canyon Creek

To Big Dry Meadow

Casa

Ninemile Creek

GOLDEN TROUT
WILDERNESS

Vieja
Meadows

To Little Dry
Meadow

To Osa Meadows

Blackrock
Gap

Blackrock Mountain ✕
9,606 ft.

SEQUOIA
NATIONAL
FOREST

21S03

N

To Blackrock Junction,
Kernville & 395

0   0.5

Miles

signed spur roads. Drive 17.2 miles beyond Sherman Pass to the three-way Blackrock Junction. The east-branching road, Forest Road 22S05, leads to Kennedy Meadows and U.S. Highway 395. Avoid this branch and continue straight ahead (north) on the paved road now bearing the Forest Road number 21S03. You quickly pass the seasonal Blackrock Ranger Station and continue north for 8.1 miles, avoiding several signed spur roads, to the Blackrock Trailhead at the road's end, 59.2 miles from Kernville.

The trail can also be reached from US 395, about 9 miles north of its junction with California 14 and 54.5 miles south of Lone Pine. Turn west on the Nine Mile Canyon/Kennedy Meadows Road; a large sign indicates Kennedy Meadows is 25 miles ahead. Follow this steadily climbing paved road up to the crest of the Sierra Nevada, and across the rolling Kern Plateau. After 25 miles, you reach a junction. Turn left (west) onto Forest Road 22S05, avoiding the northbound road, which ends in 3 miles at the Kennedy Meadows Campground. You immediately pass the Kennedy Meadows General Store, then cross the South Fork Kern River via a bridge. The road leads west for 12 miles from the Kennedy Meadows junction to Blackrock Junction, where you turn right (north) on Forest Road 21S03, and drive 8.1 miles to the trailhead.

Key points:
0.0 Blackrock Trailhead.
1.7 At the junction with the eastbound trail at Casa Vieja Meadows, stay left (northwest).

2.2 At the junction with the trail leading southwest along the west margin of Casa Vieja Meadows, bear right (north).

2.3 Reach the junction with the descending trail to Jordan Hot Springs on the north bank of Ninemile Creek.

The hike: This pleasant day hike, downhill most of the way, leads through red fir and lodgepole pine forest to the verdant, wildflower-filled spread of Casa Vieja Meadows. Surrounded by forested ridges in the heart of the Kern Plateau, the meadows give day hikers the feeling of great remoteness only 2 miles from the nearest road.

From the road's end, walk north past a corral for 0.2 mile to Blackrock Gap, where you enter the Golden Trout Wilderness. The route then descends along a tributary of Ninemile Creek for 1.5 miles, under the shade of red firs, to a junction with an eastbound trail at 1.7 miles. Continuing northwest, the trail skirts the western margin of sloping Casa Vieja Meadows, passing a southwest-branching trail at 2.2 miles, then a snow survey cabin on the left (west).

A short distance beyond the cabin, you emerge from the lodgepole pine forest to ford Ninemile Creek at the lower end of Casa Vieja Meadows. Beyond the ford at 2.3 miles, you will meet a westbound trail leading to Jordan Hot Springs, a small enclave of civilization that is the destination of the majority of hikers in this region.

The lower (western) end of the meadow, alongside Ninemile Creek, makes a fine spot to end the hike. From here, you have fine views eastward across the verdant spread while you relax alongside the golden trout-filled creek.

17
ALBANITA MEADOWS

Highlights: This easy hike leads through peaceful forests to a seldom-visited subalpine meadow on the Kern Plateau.

General location: On the west side of the Sierra Nevada in the South Sierra Wilderness and Sequoia National Forest; 70 miles northeast of Bakersfield, and 45 miles northwest of Ridgecrest.

Type of hike: Round trip.

Total distance: 4.4 miles.

Elevation gain: 200 feet.

Best months: Mid-June through October.

Maps: Sequoia National Forest map; South Sierra Wilderness and Golden Trout Wilderness topographic map; USGS Monache Mountain.

Finding the trailhead: This trail, like the trail to Casa Vieja Meadows (Hike 16), is north of Blackrock Junction. Follow the directions provided in Hike 16 to the three-way Blackrock Junction, which can be reached either from Kernville or U.S. Highway 395. At Blackrock Junction, turn right (north) onto Forest Road 21S03.

Follow Forest Road 21S03 for 3.8 miles, then turn right (northeast) onto Forest Road 21S36, where a sign indicates the Monache Jeep Road. Follow this paved road for 3.6 miles, then go right (south) where the Monache Jeep Road departs to the left (north). At the junction with southbound Forest Road 21S36A, 1.3 miles from the Monache Jeep Road junction, stay left (southeast), remaining on Forest Road 21S36. Continue for another 0.8 mile to the trailhead at the end of the road.

Key points:

0.0 The trailhead is at the end of Forest Road 21S36.
0.3 At the junction with the Albanita Trail, bear left (southeast).
0.5 Pass through the saddle at 8,800 feet.
0.8 At the junction on the saddle at the wilderness boundary, continue straight ahead (southeast).
0.9 At the junction with the eastbound trail, stay left (southeast) and begin descending.
2.0 Reach the Aqua Bonita Spring.
2.2 Arrive at the junction with the southbound Hooker Trail.

The hike: Several peaceful subalpine meadows dot the conifer-clad landscape of the South Sierra Wilderness. These grasslands are seldom visited, and the trails to them are often faint or nonexistent, but the going is easy and the camping is pleasant. Elevation gain in this area is negligible, making a hike in this part of the South Sierra Wilderness an ideal choice for novice hikers or parents with children. Because this is bear country, backpackers must make an effort to keep a clean camp and store food properly.

From the trailhead, hike southeast on the old abandoned logging trail for 0.3 mile through a forest of Jeffrey

Albanita Meadows

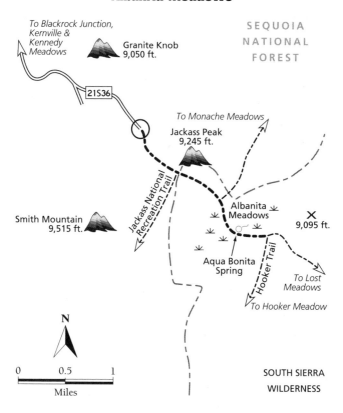

To Blackrock Junction,
Kernville &
Kennedy
Meadows

Granite Knob
9,050 ft.

SEQUOIA
NATIONAL
FOREST

21S36

To Monache Meadows

Jackass Peak
9,245 ft.

Jackass National
Recreation Trail

Smith Mountain
9,515 ft.

Albanita
Meadows

X
9,095 ft.

Aqua Bonita
Spring

Hooker Trail

To Lost
Meadows

To Hooker Meadow

N

0   0.5   1

Miles

SOUTH SIERRA
WILDERNESS

pine and red fir to the junction with the Albanita Trail,
and turn left (southeast). This trail is rarely used except by
deer and black bear.

After hiking another 0.2 mile, you reach a saddle on a ridge at 8,800 feet. From this point, you can see Jackass Peak's granite crag a short distance to the northeast. From the saddle, continue walking east on the trail, entering the South Sierra Wilderness upon cresting a low ridge at 0.8 mile and meeting the southbound Jackass National Recreation Trail on your right.

Continue southeast (straight) through thick conifers, avoiding a left-branching trail that leads northeast to Broder and Monache Meadows. Just beyond, you will drop into the bowl containing spreading Albanita Meadows. The trail here is often faint; simply follow the main trunk of the meadow eastward toward the craggy Finger Rock massif on the eastern skyline.

You will pass fenced-in Aqua Bonita Spring at 2 miles along the southern margin of this lodgepole pine-encircled spread. This is a beautiful spring, bubbling out of the sand and surrounded by a dilapidated fence that barely keeps out grazing cattle.

About 0.2 mile east of the spring, a faint tread branches south. This is the Hooker Trail, which leads over a low ridge, then drops into the infrequently visited upper reaches of Hooker Meadow after 0.75 mile (see Hike 19).

This junction marks the end of this route; from here, return to the trailhead.

18
BIG MEADOW TO MANTER MEADOW

Highlights: This memorable day hike leads to the largest meadow in the Dome Land Wilderness, a verdant spread encircled by the granodiorite domes and spires for which this wilderness area is famous.

General location: On the west side of the Sierra Nevada in the Dome Land Wilderness and Sequoia National Forest; 55 miles northeast of Bakersfield.

Type of hike: Round trip.

Total distance: 5.2 miles.

Elevation gain/loss: 460 feet/1,100 feet.

Best months: June through October.

Maps: Sequoia National Forest map; Dome Land Wilderness topographic map; USGS Sirretta Peak.

Finding the trailhead: From Kernville, proceed north along the Kern River Road (Sierra Way) for about 19 miles, then turn right (east) onto the Sherman Pass Road. Do not take the road to the left (west), which immediately crosses the Kern River and ascends into the Western Divide country.

After driving about 5.7 miles from the river, turn right (south) onto Forest Road 22S12 where a sign indicates Big Meadow. Follow this dirt road as it ascends southeast, avoiding numerous signed spur roads. You will reach a junction 9.8 miles from the Sherman Pass Road intersection.

Big Meadow to Manter Meadow

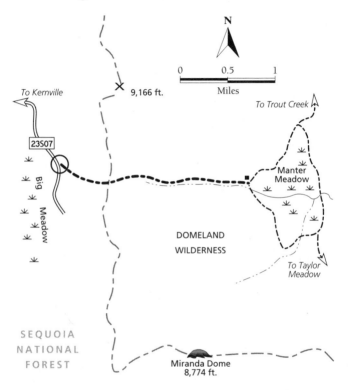

The right-hand (southeast) fork, Forest Road 22S0l, leads south along the western margin of Big Meadow, as indicated by the sign. Take the left-hand fork, Forest Road 23S07, which rises steeply at first, then proceeds for 0.7 mile to a junction at the north end of Big Meadow. Avoid the left-branching (northbound) road and continue curving south, around the northeast margin of Big Meadow, for another 0.8 mile to the signed Manter Meadow Trailhead.

Key points:

0.0 Manter Meadow Trailhead.

0.8 Enter the Dome Land Wilderness at an 8,300-foot saddle.

2.6 Reach the junction at the west end of Manter Meadow.

The hike: The awe-inspiring domes, spires, and crags of the Dome Land Wilderness, rising out of a dark green conifer forest, occupy the southern end of the Kern Plateau area. This short trip ascends a forested divide, then leads down to Manter Meadow, the largest meadow in the wilderness, and is encircled by a shady forest of pine and fir. North of Manter Meadow rises a profusion of granodiorite spires, and to the south are Miranda and Church Domes, two of the Dome Land's most prominent bedrock peaks. Cattle have been grazed here for generations, and you may see a herd grazing in Manter Meadow, usually from about July through September.

From the trailhead, follow the well-worn trail southeast up a gentle grade into a forested draw. Here, the trail rises eastward at a moderate grade, following the track of a skid trail created when this area was selectively logged many years ago. The trail tops out at the Dome Land Wilderness boundary on a saddle at 8,300 feet, 0.8 mile from the trailhead.

From the saddle, the trail descends 1,100 feet through pine and fir forest, following an ever-deepening draw that supports a sluggish, seasonal flow of water. At 2.6 miles, pass a small cabin used in summer by the holder of the area's grazing allotment permit. Just beyond the cabin, you will reach the trail junction that marks the end of this route.

Option: You can also follow trails that loop around the meadow, adding 3.3 miles to the hike. Although the best views open up from the east margin of the meadow where Manter Creek enters a narrow canyon, you will enjoy excellent views by leaving the trail near the cabin and heading east through the forest to the meadow's edge. The trails that lead left (northeast) and right (southeast) at the junction stay inside the forest, and offer only tree-framed vignettes of the surrounding domes.

19
HOOKER MEADOW

Highlights: This short hike surveys typically peaceful land-scapes of the Kern Plateau. The trail leads through pine and fir forests to the long green spread of Hooker Meadow, where one of the most extensive aspen stands on the Kern Plateau is found.

General location: On the west side of the Sierra Nevada in the South Sierra Wilderness and Sequoia National Forest; 70 miles northeast of Bakersfield, and 45 miles northwest of Ridgecrest.

Type of hike: Round trip.

Total distance: 4 to 7 miles.

Elevation gain: 700 to 800 feet.

Best months: June through October.

Maps: Sequoia National Forest map; South Sierra Wilderness and Golden Trout Wilderness topographic map; USGS Crag Peak.

Finding the trailhead: From Kernville, drive about 19 miles up the Kern River Road (Sierra Way), then turn right (east) onto Sherman Pass Road (Forest Road 41/22S05). This road quickly climbs eastward out of Kern River canyon, surmounts Sherman Pass 14.4 miles from the river, and continues east, then north, passing numerous signed spur roads. You will reach the three-way Blackrock Junction 17.2 miles beyond Sherman Pass.

Hooker Meadow

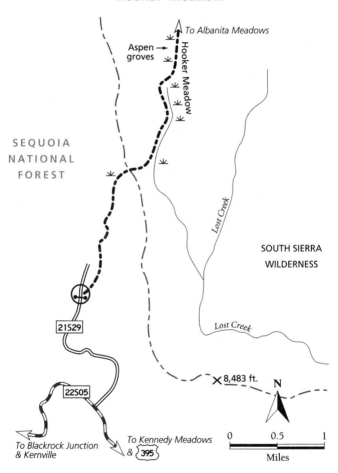

To Albanita Meadows

Aspen groves

Hooker Meadow

SEQUOIA NATIONAL FOREST

Lost Creek

SOUTH SIERRA WILDERNESS

Lost Creek

21S29

22S05

✕ 8,483 ft.

N

To Blackrock Junction & Kernville

To Kennedy Meadows & 395

0   0.5   1

Miles

From the junction, follow the eastbound Forest Road 22S05 toward Kennedy Meadows and U.S. Highway 395 for another 5 miles, then turn left (northeast) onto Forest Road 21S29, signed "Hooker Trail 1.5." This is a fair dirt road, rutted and rocky in places. Pass a corral and loading chute after 0.6 mile; the Hooker Trailhead is at a gate 1.9 miles from the intersection with Forest Road 22S05.

From US 395, about 10 miles north of its junction with California 14, and 54.5 miles south of Lone Pine, turn west onto the Nine Mile Canyon/Kennedy Meadows Road; a large sign indicates Kennedy Meadows is 25 miles ahead. Follow this steadily climbing paved road up to the crest of the Sierra and across the Kern Plateau. After 25 miles you will reach a junction. Turn left (west) onto Forest Road 22S05, avoiding the northbound road, which ends in 3 miles at the Kennedy Meadows Campground. Pass the Kennedy Meadows General Store, then cross the South Fork Kern River via a bridge after 0.9 mile. From the river, Sherman Pass Road ascends into pine forest, and after another 7 miles, reaches the unpaved Forest Road 21S29. Turn right (northeast), and drive 1.9 miles to the Hooker Trailhead.

Key points:
0.0 Trailhead.
2.0 Reach the western margin of Hooker Meadow.
3.5 Arrive at the upper reaches of the meadow.

The hike: The trail to Hooker Meadow is one of the best and most easily accessible trails in the South Sierra Wilderness.

Hooker Meadow is an attractive and popular destination in the summer, but much less frequently used in the autumn, when its extensive groves of aspen reach the peak of their brilliant colors. Most hikers follow only the first 2 miles of the trail to the western margin of 2-mile-long meadow. For more solitude and an opportunity to enjoy the aspen groves, follow the gradually ascending trail for another 1.5 miles toward the north end of the meadow.

From the trailhead, the well-worn Hooker Trail leads gradually uphill along an unnamed, seasonal tributary of Fish Creek. Park-like stands of Jeffrey pine, mixed with white fir and Sierra juniper, dominate the forest, and clumps of manzanita inhabit sunny openings. The first mile follows the path of a retired logging road and passes the stumps of trees selectively cut from the forest.

The trail requires three easy "jump-across" fords of the small stream in the first 1.5 miles. The third crossing lies at the southern end of a small, corn lily-fringed meadow, where the trail is obscure. Several yards beyond a very large blowdown lodgepole pine, look for the well-worn trail ascending a moderate grade away from the drainage, first northeast, then east. The trail rises through a Jeffrey pine forest to a broad ridge where you enter the South Sierra Wilderness.

From the ridge, you descend an almost imperceptible grade to a soggy arm of Hooker Meadow. Curve northeast around a low, forested ridge to the western margin of the meadow near its southern end, which is about 8,300 feet and 2 miles from the trailhead. You can either backtrack to the trailhead from here, or continue northward.

If you choose to continue, follow the trail generally north along the western margins of the meadow, where the trail is well defined in the pine forest, but faint in the open grasslands. As you approach what appears to be the upper, northern end of the meadow, where the grasslands are pinched into a pine-fringed, sagebrush-clad draw, cross over to the eastern side and enter the upper reaches of Hooker Meadow. Aspen groves, some of the most extensive on the Kern Plateau, fringe the meadow here, about 3.5 miles from the trailhead.

20
SOUTH FORK KERN RIVER

Highlights: This pleasant hike follows a segment of the Pacific Crest Trail through pinyon and juniper woodlands along the South Fork Kern River.

General location: On the west side of the Sierra Nevada in the Sequoia National Forest, the Bureau of Land Management's Ridgecrest Resource Area, and the Dome Land Wilderness; 40 miles northwest of Ridgecrest, and 58 miles northeast of Bakersfield.

Type of hike: Round trip.

Total distance: 4 miles or more.

Elevation gain: Negligible.

Best months: May and June; mid-September to October.

Maps: Sequoia National Forest map; Dome Land Wilderness topographic map; USGS Crag Peak and Rockhouse Basin.

Finding the trailhead: To reach the trailhead from Kernville, drive about 19 miles up the Kern River Road (Sierra Way) then turn right (east) onto Sherman Pass Road (Forest Road 41/22S05). This road quickly climbs eastward out of the Kern River canyon. The road crests Sherman Pass 14.4 miles from the river; drive 17.2 miles from Sherman Pass to the three-way Blackrock Junction. Follow the eastbound Forest Road 22S05 toward Kennedy Meadows and U.S. Highway 395. You eventually descend to the bridge span-

South Fork Kern River

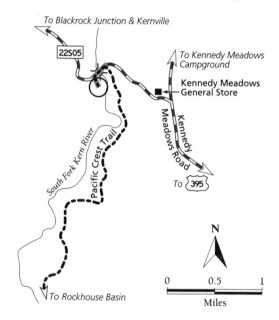

To Blackrock Junction & Kernville

22S05

To Kennedy Meadows
Campground

Kennedy Meadows
General Store

South Fork Kern River

Pacific Crest Trail

Kennedy Meadows Road

To 395

To Rockhouse Basin

N

0   0.5   1
Miles

ning the South Fork Kern River, 12 miles from Blackrock
Junction. Turn right (south) at the west end of the bridge
and drive a few hundred yards to the trailhead parking area.

To reach the trailhead from US 395, about 10 miles
north of its junction with California 14, and 54.5 miles
south of Lone Pine, turn west onto the Nine Mile
Canyon/Kennedy Meadows Road. Follow this paved road
to the crest of the Sierra and across the Kern Plateau. At
the 25 mile-mark, you will reach a junction. Turn left

(west) onto Forest Road 22S05, avoiding the right (north-bound) road. Pass the Kennedy Meadows General Store, then cross the South Fork Kern River via a bridge after 0.9 mile. Park at the trailhead a few hundred yards south of the road, on the west side of the river.

The hike: This fine segment of the Pacific Crest Trail (PCT) along the South Fork Kern River leads nearly 7 miles to the broad valley of Rockhouse Basin, and features inspiring views into the Dome Land Wilderness. It also boasts productive fishing for brown and rainbow trout. The trip has no particular destination other than the river itself, which is accessible from many points along the trail. The first 2 miles of the nearly level trail afford the best river access.

From the trailhead parking area, walk back to the paved road and head east across the bridge. You will find the southbound PCT immediately above (east of) the east abutment of the bridge. The trail follows a gentle, undulating course across corrugated slopes above the east bank of the river. Beware of rattlesnakes; they are abundant here.

The first few miles closely follow the wilderness boundary, delineated by a fence line, with private property and an occasional residence just beyond. During the first few miles, the river is close by, and inspiring views stretch into the domed landscape to the southwest as well as into the broad canyon of Trout Creek.

You must leave the trail to reach the banks of the river. Be careful; during late spring and early summer, the river runs high and swift, and can be very dangerous. When you've hiked as far as you wish, return as you came.